Wilma Rudolph

by Corinne J. Naden and Rose Blue

Raintree

Chicago, Illinois

JB RUDOLPH

© 2004 Raintree
Published by Raintree, a division of Reed Elsevier, Inc.
Chicago, Illinois
Customer Service: 888-363-4266
Visit our website at www.raintreelibrary.com

For information, address the publisher:
Raintree, 100 N. LaSalle, Suite 1200, Chicago, IL 60602

Printed and bound in the United States at Lake Book Manufacturing, Inc.
07 06 05 04 03
10 9 8 7 6 5 4 3 2 1

Library of Congress Cataloging-in-Publication Data:

Naden, Corinne J.
  Wilma Rudolph / Corinne J. Naden and Rose Blue.
    p. cm. -- (African-American biographies)
Summary: Profiles Wilma Rudolph, a sickly child born to a poor family in rural Tennessee who went on to become a world famous, record-breaking, Olympic track star.
Includes bibliographical references and index.
  ISBN 0-7398-7033-5 (Library Binding-hardcover) -- ISBN 1-4109-0321-4 (Paperback)
  1. Rudolph, Wilma, 1940---Juvenile literature. 2. Runners (Sports)--United States--Biography--Juvenile literature. 3. Women runners--United States--Biography--Juvenile literature. [1. Rudolph, Wilma, 1940- 2. Track and field athletes. 3. African Americans--Biography. 4. Women--Biography.] I. Blue, Rose. II. Title. III. Series.
  GV1061.15.R83N33 2003
  796.42'092--dc21

                          2003006140

Acknowledgments
The publisher would like to thank the following for permission to reproduce photographs:
pp. 4, 8, 19, 23, 40, 47, 48, 51 Library of Congress; pp. 6, 10, 12, 16, 28, 32, 34, 37, 38, 43, 45, 52, 54, 57 Bettmann/Corbis; p. 14 Steve Raymer/Corbis; pp. 20, 26 Hulton/Archive by Getty Images; p. 31 Associated Press, AP.

Cover Photograph: Bettmann/Corbis

Some words are shown in bold, **like this.** You can find out what they mean by looking in the glossary.

Contents

Wilma Rudolph was one of the fastest runners the world had ever seen. She runs here at a track meet in 1961.

Introduction

Wilma Rudolph was one of the best runners in the world. She ran so fast and broke so many records that she was known as the "fastest woman in the world." She was also very graceful, and newspaper reporters around the world often wrote about her.

Wilma's story is amazing, but not just because she grew up to be a talented athlete. It is amazing that she could run at all. Sickly and small at birth, young Wilma fought illnesses and poor health throughout her childhood. This did not stop her. Wilma was determined to run. She once said, "I don't know why I run so fast; I just run."

Poor health was not the only obstacle to Wilma's success. She also had to overcome **segregation.** Under segregation, rules or laws unfairly forced black people to live apart from white people in the United States. Blacks had to have their own schools, hospitals, and neighborhoods. These things were never nearly as good as they

Wilma smiles for the camera in 1968. After winning three gold medals in the 1960 Olympic Games in Rome, she worked for anti-poverty and civil rights organizations.

were for white people. African-American schools did not receive as much money or equipment as white schools. This meant that the schools did not have as many sports opportunities or extra programs. There were not many black doctors, and the hospitals that existed for black people didn't have new equipment or the best medicines. Wilma wanted to help change this.

To do this, Wilma worked for anti-**poverty** and **civil rights** organizations. She created a foundation to help talented young athletes. Through her hard work and courage, Wilma Rudolph taught thousands of young Americans a valuable lesson. The way to win is never, never to quit trying. She once said, "The triumph can't be had without the struggle."

In her own words

"Never underestimate the power of dreams and the influence of the human spirit. We are all the same in this notion: The potential for greatness lives within each of us."

"My mother taught me very early to believe I could achieve any accomplishment I wanted to. The first was to walk without braces."

"When I was going through my transition of being famous, I tried to ask God, Why was I here? What was my purpose? Surely, it wasn't just to win three gold medals. There has to be more to this life than that."

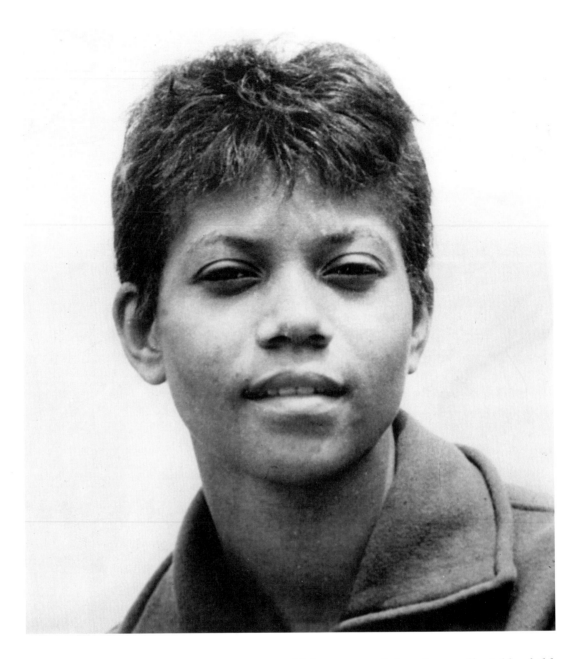

Wilma was born June 23, 1940. No one could have guessed that the small, sickly child would grow up to be such an amazing runner. She is shown here at age twenty.

Chapter 1:
Growing Up in Tennessee

When Wilma Glodean Rudolph was born on June 23, 1940, no one expected her to live. She weighed only four and one-half pounds. At the time, babies born that small usually did not survive. An average newborn baby usually weighs between six and eight pounds.

Wilma was born in rural St. Bethlehem, Tennessee, to a family that was poor and African American. There was only one African-American doctor in town. Because of **segregation** laws, Wilma had to go to a special hospital that treated African Americans. The closest hospital that treated African-American patients was Meharry Hospital, which was staffed by the African-American medical college of Fisk University. Meharry Hospital was in Nashville, 50 miles away from St. Bethlehem.

The South practiced segregation when Wilma was growing up. There were separate things—such as schools, bathrooms, and drinking fountains—for whites and blacks to use.

Poor and black

Tiny Wilma did live. She was the twentieth of twenty-two children in the Rudolph family. Her father, Ed, was a porter and handyman. A porter carries baggage for people. His second wife and Wilma's mother, Blanche, worked as a maid and a cook, and also did other people's laundry. Her parents worked hard, but they earned very little money. The children wore hand-me-down clothes. Wilma's mother made some clothes for her daughters out of old flour sacks. The Rudolph house had no electricity, no running water, and no bathroom. There was an outhouse, or outdoor toilet, near the back door.

The Rudolphs moved to Clarksville, Tennessee, soon after Wilma was born. The town was mostly white. Life in the 1940s was hard for most black families in the South. There were not many jobs. Most of the good-paying jobs went to white people. African Americans who could find jobs often did not earn much money. Because of **segregation** laws, blacks could eat at only one restaurant in town. They had to drink from separate water fountains. They had to go to blacks-only schools that were not funded as well as whites-only schools.

To make matters worse, Wilma Rudolph was a sickly child. She came down with everything—mumps, measles, chicken pox. There were no shots against those diseases at the time. Her parents could not have afforded them anyway. Then, she got double pneumonia and scarlet fever. When she finally recovered from all those illnesses, her mother noticed something wrong with Wilma's leg. Her left leg was suddenly crooked and the foot turned inward. The doctors thought Wilma had contracted **polio** when she was sick for so long. Polio is a disease that attacks nerves in the spinal cord and brain stem, often causing paralysis. Today, there is a **vaccine** for polio. But back then, polio killed many children and paralyzed thousands of others.

In the South, one of the laws of segregation required that African Americans sit at the rear of the buses. The Supreme Court ordered the buses desegregated in 1956.

The long road back

To get better, Wilma's leg had to be treated twice a week in a hospital. But **segregation** was still in place, and the Clarksville hospital did not treat black people. So in 1946, the long trips began to the all-black Meharry Medical College. Twice a week, Wilma and her mother took the Greyhound bus for the 100-mile round trip. They had to sit in the blacks-only seats at the rear of the bus unless white people were sitting in them. In that case, they had to stand. That was especially hard on Wilma because she had to wear a heavy leg brace. It was hard for her to stand so long.

In Nashville, Wilma sat in a whirlpool tub. **Therapists** massaged her leg. She had to do exercises to make her leg stronger. Eventually, the doctors taught her mother how to do the massages and exercises at home. After two years, Wilma did not have to make the long trip twice a week anymore.

Her mother and her brothers and sisters helped Wilma do her treatment at home. She was too sick to attend school, so she was tutored at home. This routine went on for years. It was hard work and it was painful. It was also lonely. Because of her leg, she did not start school until she was seven. Then, she began attending the second grade at the all-black Cobb Elementary School. But she could not do what the other children did. She could not jump or skip or play ball.

Because she was lonely, Wilma had a lot of time to think. She saw the way black people were treated on buses and in restaurants. These feelings made her angry. She vowed that one day she would fight against unequal treatment because of one's skin color. And she also vowed that one day she would walk like anybody else.

Wilma had to wear a leg brace such as these when she was growing up. She could not run or play games because of the brace.

Wilma not only wanted to walk, but she wanted to play some of the sports that other children played. So she worked hard at her exercises every day, and she tried to ignore the pain. At night she would take off her brace to see if her leg looked any straighter. But it still looked crooked.

Even so, Wilma's family tried to help her by saying that her leg looked straighter. At least, that made her feel better.

Free at last

Then one day it happened. Wilma was about nine and a half years old. She took off the leg brace and walked outside, just like that. Then she walked into church. She later said it was the most important day of her life. From then on, she spent some time in the leg brace and some time out of the brace to build up her strength. By 1950 her mother mailed the leg brace back to Nashville. Wilma was ten years old. But Wilma's pain and hard work were not over. She had to keep up the exercises for two more years before her leg was straight.

After her leg healed, she could think about something more than just walking. She could think about being just like anyone else. And for twelve-year-old Wilma Rudolph, that meant playing basketball.

Wilma always dreamed she would be able to run or play sports with the other kids. Her positive attitude and her determination helped her deal with everything life dealt her. By the age of 21, she had already won three gold medals in the Olympic Games.

Chapter 2:
A Natural Athlete

Wilma Rudolph just loved basketball. During all the years that she could not play games and sports, she would watch the other children shooting a ball through an old rim nailed on a barn. Many times she dreamed of racing down the court and making a basket. By the time she was twelve years old and in seventh grade, she was ready for basketball. That year, she entered Burt High School, which was for students in grades seven through twelve. Wilma signed up for the basketball team and began attending practices.

Making the team

Coach Clinton Gray put Rudolph's name on the player list. Soon after joining, she began to show speed and smoothness on the court. She got the nickname of "Skeeter," because she buzzed around the court so much like a mosquito. Yet, no matter how much she improved, Wilma spent most of the time sitting on the bench. Still, she kept on practicing.

In the off season, she began to run on the girls' track team that Coach Gray had started. Wilma liked that and she was good at it, generally beating out all the other runners. Wilma was very thin, and she had also grown tall. She now stood about five feet eleven inches, and her legs were long and muscular.

Finally her basketball dream came true in the first game of her tenth grade. Coach Gray made her a starting guard. She later said she was the happiest person in the whole state of Tennessee that night. In her first start, Wilma scored an amazing 32 points. After that, she was a permanent starter.

Someone watching

The basketball season was over, so Wilma turned to track. Then one day in 1956, she went to the track meet sponsored by the Amateur Athletic Union (AAU). It was held at Tuskegee Institute in Alabama, and it was her first time on a college campus. Wilma still figured she would win easily, just as she always had.

That proved to be one of the worst nights of Rudolph's life. She did not win a single race. For a long time, she felt bad about Tuskegee, but she did not quit running. She said later that the greatest lesson at Tuskegee was that it taught her how to lose. She learned not to dwell on a loss. Instead, she decided to learn from the mistakes she made, and to train and try harder for the next race.

In 1956 Wilma competed in a track meet at Tuskegee Institute in Alabama (pictured). At Tuskegee, Wilma learned a valuable lesson—how to lose.

At the end of the season, Coach Gray had some news. Ed Temple had been watching her. He was the coach of the Tigerbelles at Tennessee State University. They were one of the best and most famous women's sports teams in the United States.

Temple wanted to talk to Wilma's parents. He hoped they would give permission for Wilma to spend the summer at Tennessee State training with other talented high school athletes. Temple thought Wilma could be a champion runner.

Wilma practiced starts with her teammates. She always felt that her starts needed to improve for her to win races.

Chapter 3: Training Time

Wilma Rudolph could not believe her luck. Her parents accepted Coach Temple's offer to let her train at Tennessee State for the summer. She felt sad about leaving her family and her friends, but Coach Temple had given her a wonderful opportunity.

Back to basics

Wilma discovered a whole new world at Tennessee State. She learned new ways of training to build her strength. She and the other girls ran twenty miles a day, five days a week. The coach explained that **cross-country** running would help her to be at her best during an entire race. Cross-country means running a certain distance over open country, instead of running on a track. She learned to breathe freely and naturally while running.

Wilma also learned that she could never entirely beat one problem—starting a race. Many races are lost because a runner does not have a good, fast start. Wilma said that she felt like her legs were too long. It took a few wobbly strides for her to get in rhythm. To make up for this, she began running in longer races. She had learned that she would always do better in longer races so that she had time to make up for a slow start.

Going up north

In August during that summer of 1956, Coach Temple took the team on Wilma's first trip north for an AAU track and field event. She nearly fainted when she entered the stadium at Franklin Field at the University of Pennsylvania in Philadelphia. She had never before seen a place so big. It made her nervous. But she did not act nervous on the track. She entered nine races and won them all. Wilma gained a lot of confidence at this track event in Philadelphia.

While in Philadelphia, Wilma met and had her picture taken with baseball hero Jackie Robinson. He was the first black player in organized baseball when he joined the then–Brooklyn Dodgers in 1947. Before that time, black Americans could not play baseball with white Americans. They played in a separate league with poorer equipment and less money. It was not easy for Robinson to be the first, but his courage and talent helped remove the **color barrier** in baseball. Robinson told Wilma that he liked her style. He told her to keep on running. She never forgot that meeting with Robinson. He became her hero.

Jackie Robinson

Jackie Robinson (1919–1972) is known for being the first African-American baseball player in the U.S. major leagues. He played professional baseball for the Brooklyn Dodgers from 1947 to 1956. At first, many people did not like the idea of **integrating** major league baseball. Robinson had to endure much **racism.** But his natural talent and his easy-going personality won him many

fans. Today, Robinson is known for being one of baseball's greatest players. He was Rookie of the Year in 1947. He won the National League Most Valuable Player in 1949. He retired from baseball in 1957 and was elected to the Baseball Hall of Fame in 1962. He died in 1972.

Olympic dreams

Wilma got back to Clarksville and felt like a hero herself. Her family and friends were thrilled that she had done so well. Now she got an even bigger thrill.

Coach Temple talked to her about the Olympic Games. Wilma did not even know what they were. Temple explained that every

The Olympics

The Olympic Games were first held at Olympia in ancient Greece in 776 B.C. The games were revived by Baron Pierre de Coubertin of France during the 1800s. The modern Olympic Games honor the world's best in fair play, skill, and sportsmanship. Except during World Wars I and II, the Games have been held in different cities around the world every four years.

Nations put together and send Olympic teams to compete in the games. Each amateur athlete represents his or her country. The grand prize in each event is the gold medal, followed by silver and bronze medals for second and third places. To honor the athlete and his or her country, the flag and national anthem of the gold-medal winner is played at a special medal-awards ceremony following each event. To win the gold medal means that the athlete is considered to be the best in the world at his or her sport. It is probably the most respected prize in sports.

Today the Games are now separated into summer and winter events. Summer Games have many sporting events, including archery, basketball, boxing, diving, fencing, gymnastics, rowing, swimming, and tennis. Some events in the Winter Games are bobsled, ice hockey, ski jumping, ice skating, and skiing.

four years the Olympic Games are held in a different world city. It is a great honor to be chosen to compete for one's country in the Olympic Games. Only the best of each country's amateur athletes are chosen to compete in these games every four years. To win in the Olympics means that the athlete is judged to be the best in the world at his or her sport.

Temple told Wilma that the 1956 Games were set for Melbourne, Australia. That meant little to Wilma because she had no idea where Melbourne was. She learned it was halfway around the world. Then the coach said something truly exciting. He wanted her to compete in the 1956 Games. But first she would have to qualify at the Olympic **Trials** in Seattle, Washington.

Now a high school junior and age sixteen, Wilma traveled to Seattle with a group of older college track stars, including Mae Faggs. Wilma was so nervous, she was sure she would never get out of the starting block. Wilma later said that Mae, the most experienced runner on the team, encouraged Wilma and was a great boost to her confidence.

Wilma tied the veteran Mae in the first trial heat of the 200 meters. And they both made the team. Wilma was sixteen years old. Just a few years earlier, she could not even walk without a leg brace, let alone run. Now she was the youngest member on the U.S. women's track team.

Wilma takes a breather after running a record-breaking 11.3-second 100-meter dash.
She competed at this American-Soviet track-and-field event in July 1961.

Chapter 4:
The 1956 Olympics

Wilma flew in a plane for the first time from Nashville heading for Los Angeles, California, to begin her Olympic training. She arrived with new clothes and new luggage as a gift from local store owners in her hometown. She later said that what she mostly remembered about Los Angeles was the smog. It was so bad that she hardly saw the city.

For two weeks, Wilma and the team trained at the University of Southern California. The coach of the U.S. women's track team was Nel Jackson, the first-ever black women's coach for the U.S. Olympic team. During those two weeks, Wilma gained a lot of confidence in her ability. She was excited about her chances in the 200-meter run. And she was especially excited about being part of the four-member **relay** team.

Wilma's teammate, Mae Faggs of New York, did not let the fall of Leela Rao from India distract her from the race. She placed third in the first heat of the 100-meter race of the 1956 Olympics.

In a **relay** race, the first runner finishes a leg of the race, for example, one lap around the track. Then she passes the **baton** to the second runner as they both run along the track. The second passes the baton to the third and the third to the fourth. The fourth runner, who finishes the race, is called the **anchor.** Relay teams often put their best runners at anchor in case the team is behind at that point. Wilma was running in the number three spot on the team, Mae Faggs was first. The other team members were Margaret Matthews, running second, and Isabelle Daniels as the anchor.

On to Melbourne

After training, the team left on a two-day flight to Melbourne, Australia. To Wilma, everything was new and exciting. After a stop in Hawaii, they landed in the Fiji Islands in the South Pacific. Wilma was amazed at an island filled with black people, and not one of them spoke English. She began to understand what Mae Faggs had told her, that traveling with an Olympic team means a lot more education than just sports. She was seeing places and people she had never imagined before.

At last Wilma reached Melbourne. It was October, which is summertime in Australia. The team checked into the Olympic Village, where the athletes stay while they are competing. Wilma felt comfortable there. Everybody seemed to get along no matter what their skin color was. People on the street asked her for her autograph. Athletes in the Olympics are always big stars during the games. But she was not yet big news in the United States.

The Olympic Games

On the third day of the games, a confident Wilma ran her first race. It was the trial run for the 200-meter dash. The first three finishers go to the semifinals. Wilma finished third. She qualified, but this time only the first two finishers would go to the finals.

Wilma finished third. She was out of the 200-meter race. That night, she felt so bad that she could not eat or sleep. She felt she had let down everyone back home. Wilma told herself that she would work really hard for the next four years. And she decided then that she would win the gold medal for the United States.

Still, Wilma still had the **relay** race ahead of her at the 1956 Games. She was ready to do her best. The U.S. relay team, however, was not expected to get a medal. The all-important part of a relay is passing the baton. It has to be quick and smooth. Wilma and her teammates just could not get the timing right.

The race began with Faggs on the first lap. When she passed the baton to Matthews, the U.S. team was tied for first. But when Matthews passed the baton to Wilma for the third lap, the team was several places behind. Wilma ran as she never had before. When the anchor got the baton for the last lap, the team was in third place. And that is where they finished. The United States won a bronze medal. Next time, Wilma thought, it will be a gold medal.

Back in high school

Wilma returned to being just another high school student. This time, however, it was different. Her friends and teammates treated her differently. The fact that she was a star athlete set her apart from them. Some people were jealous. Others acted as though they were afraid to be themselves around her. But after a while, they began to relax and treat her like the old Wilma. She also suffered a great tragedy that year. Wilma and her boyfriend, Robert Eldridge,

Wilma posed with her teammates after they placed third and received a bronze medal in the 4 x 100-meter relay. From left are Margaret Matthews, Wilma, Mae Faggs, and Isabelle Daniels.

went to the Junior-Senior Prom with other friends. Later that night, Wilma's best friend, Nancy Bowen, was killed in a car accident. Wilma remembered that time with great sadness.

At the end of May 1958, Rudolph graduated from high school. She had won a full athletic **scholarship** to Tennessee State and the Tigerbelles. The Tigerbelles were famous for winning many sporting events.

Wilma was happy after she set a new American women's indoor record at the Los Angeles Invitational. She used her hands to demonstrate how much she had won the race by.

Chapter 5:
On to Tennessee State

Wilma Rudolph moved to Nashville to attend college at Tennessee State University in the fall of 1958. She was eighteen years old.

If Wilma thought she had worked hard before, she had not even begun. Coach Temple did not mold a great women's sports team by being soft. The young women had to train and train hard. They had to run an extra lap around the track for every minute they were late to practice. Once, Wilma was half an hour late. She had to run an extra 30 laps around the track. She was never that late again!

The athletes also had study hard. To stay on the Tigerbelles meant keeping at least a B average in the classroom. Wilma studied elementary education at Tennessee. She thought she might be a teacher after her sports career.

Wilma breaks through the ribbon to set a new world's record in the 200-meter race at the National Women's Amateur Athletics Union track and field meet. She was 19 years old.

Hard work

This was work such as Wilma had never known. But she was determined. When the training and studying got tough, she thought about her dream—winning the gold medal in the Olympics. That dream kept her focused throughout the difficult times.

Even though the work was hard, Wilma's freshman year in college went well. Wilma made the track team and was its fastest runner. However, she still could not get off the starting block in a hurry. It was a weakness she just could not correct. But she was lucky in that she usually could make up for the poor start with her terrific speed down the track.

The Nationals

Whenever she had the time, Wilma's mind jumped to the 1960 Olympics in Rome, Italy. First, she would have to do well at the National AAU meet in Corpus Christi, Texas. The best competitors at the AAU meet would be invited to the Olympic **Trials** at Texas Christian University in Fort Worth. The trials are tryouts for the Olympics. Wilma would have to qualify at the Olympic Trials. Winners of the first three places in the Trials go to the Olympic Games. Wilma was confident she could do well at both.

On the bus to Corpus Christi, Rudolph felt the **racism** that was a large part of life in the 1950s and 1960s. The driver refused to drive the bus to the meet because it carried both black and white students. Another driver had to be found who would drive an **integrated** bus.

This was just one of many times that Wilma had seen and felt **racism.** It hurt her deeply. However, she never talked openly about the pain. Later in life, she would work to help others who were victims of racism. But Wilma did not let racism and **segregation** affect her running. She did not think of herself as a black athlete or a female athlete. She wanted to be known only as an athlete.

Wilma did very well at the Nationals and again at the Olympic Trials. In fact, she ran the 200-meter race in 22.9 seconds, the fastest ever run by a woman. It was a world record, and it was not broken for eight years.

At the trials, Wilma also won the 100-meter dash. On top of that, she qualified for the **relay** and easily made the Olympic team, as did three other Tigerbelles.

The U.S. track team traveled from Texas to Kansas State University in Emporia to begin training. Before they arrived in Kansas, they found out who would be coach of the Olympic track team that year. It was none other than Ed Temple of Tennessee State. Wilma was thrilled. What could be better than having her college coach train her for the Olympics?

Training time again

Wilma liked training at Kansas State. The living quarters were very nice, and so was the track. Wilma also loved the food. While she was there, she ate some of the biggest steaks she had ever seen!

In 1958 Wilma posed with the other future 1960 Olympians. She is second from left in the second row. Mae Faggs is fourth from left in the same row.

Wilma puts on her warm-up sweats and her lucky straw hat just after she won her third gold medal of the 1960 Olympic Games in Rome, Italy.

Coach Temple worked the young women hard in training. They ran three times a day. Wilma was tall, and she was underweight for her size. So, Temple cut her practices down to twice and then once a day, so she would not burn herself out before the Olympics.

By the end of the training period, Wilma felt really good about herself and her chances. She knew she had a chance to win three gold medals in Rome. If she did not win them, she told herself, it would be her fault alone. She was in great shape, and her coach was with her. Wilma knew she could do it.

The Tennessee Tigerbelles pose together after setting the new world record for the 400-meter relay in the 1960 Olympics. From left are Wilma, Lucinda Williams, Barbara Jones, and Martha Hudson.

Chapter 6:
The 1960 Olympics

The ancient city of Rome, Italy, was in the middle of a heat wave. The 6,000 athletes for the 1960 Games arrived in 100° F (38° C) temperatures. That may have bothered the young people from the cold country of Norway, but it certainly did not bother the Tigerbelles. Temperatures like these were normal for a summer in Tennessee.

After a week's stay in New York City, the team settled in at the Olympic Village in Rome. For Wilma, it was like seeing all her history book pictures come to life. There was the Vatican where the Pope lived, and the Coliseum where the gladiators fought the lions in ancient times. The Italian people were friendly and seemed genuinely to enjoy having the athletes there.

Almost disaster

The day before Wilma's first race, the team practiced on a green field behind Olympic Stadium. It was green because it was covered with water sprinklers. Wilma caught her foot in a hole behind one of the sprinklers. She heard a popping noise and started to cry.

Everyone ran over to help her. All Wilma could do was stare at the ankle that had quickly swollen. The coach called for some ice. Wilma was terrified that she had broken her ankle and would not be able to run. Suddenly she saw all her work and all her Olympic dreams go down that sprinkler hole.

The trainer taped her ankle and carried her to her room. Wilma kept her foot propped up all night, afraid to find out how bad it was. In the morning, she carefully put her foot on the floor. She could stand. It was only a sprain. Wilma figured she could run, and still win, with a sprain. A sprain is a stretching or tearing of the tissue that connects bones to joints, such as the ankle. It can be very painful.

In the meantime, word of the accident had spread around the Olympic Village. Everyone thought that Wilma Rudolph would not be racing. People thought she had broken her ankle.

Only Wilma knew that she could run. The next day, she walked into the tunnel that led to Olympic Stadium. She sat

Wilma crossed the finish line of a women's sprint event at the 1960 Olympics. She had sprained her ankle the previous day, but she did not let that stop her from chasing the gold.

with her foot propped against a wall, waiting for her name to be called. All she could think about was the gold medal.

Then she heard her name called and walked out into a crowd of 80,000 people. She heard their loud cheers. They were obviously delighted to see her walking. Keeping her mind focused, Wilma easily won the two trial heats of the day. Her ankle did not bother her. On the next day, she won the third heat easily. In the fourth heat, she set a new world's record—11 seconds. However, the Olympic Committee would not let the record stand. They said the wind at her back was more than 2.2 miles per hour. If judges think the wind pushes a runner and makes him or her run faster than usual, a winning record may be disqualified. Coach Temple told her not to be upset. The most important race was on Saturday.

Going for gold

The 100-meter women's final on Saturday had six competitors. Wilma came out of the start second or third, which for her was a fast takeoff. Wilma took the 100 meters by about seven yards. Once again she ran it in 11 seconds flat. Unfortunately, the record was not allowed because of the wind. That did not matter to Wilma when she stood up to take her first gold medal.

Tuesday was the 200-meter race. Her ankle was holding up well. The day started out with rain, but Wilma did not mind. She felt she could win anything. And she was right. She won once again with a time of 24 seconds. She had two gold medals, and there was still one race left.

The 4 X 100-meter **relay** was to take place on Friday. If the relay team won, she would become the first U.S. woman ever to win three gold medals at one Olympics. However, the U.S. relay team was not expected to win. Great Britain, West Germany, and what was then known as the Soviet Union were supposed to be faster. Wilma told herself not to worry about them.

Wilma runs the anchor, or end part, of the relay and crosses the finish line ahead of Russia's Irina Press to claim her third gold medal. No U.S. woman had ever won that many gold medals in one Olympics.

The U.S. relay team placed Barbara Hudson on the first leg, followed by Barbara Jones and Lucinda Williams, with Wilma running anchor. It was important to get a fast start. Hudson and Jones did their job. When Williams came charging down the track to hand the baton to the anchor, the U.S. team was leading. But as Wilma reached out to grab the baton, she nearly dropped it. She struggled to regain control, but by then, the German and Soviet runners had passed her. Angry with herself for her mistake, Wilma pushed her body to run as fast as she could.

As she neared the finish line, she trailed the German runner by two meters. One last great lunge sent Wilma through the tape. Not only did the U.S. team win, by three-tenths of a second, but also they set a new world record of 44.5 seconds. This time it was official; the wind was not a problem.

It was a very special moment for 20-year-old Wilma Rudolph, the once-sickly girl from Tennessee. She was famous. She was an Olympic medalist. People called her the "Tennessee Tornado." Best of all, they called her the fastest woman in the world.

Wilma had fans all around the world. After the Olympics, the U.S. team traveled to Greece, England, Holland, and Germany. When the team was in Berlin, Germany, fans surrounded and pounded on the team's bus until Wilma waved to them.

Fighting segregation

It was a happy Wilma Rudolph who returned home. Clarksville held a ceremony in Wilma's honor. There was even a parade.

Wilma used this chance to fight against **segregation.** In 1954 the U.S. Supreme Court declared segregated schools to be against the law. But it took many years before segregation was gone from schools and restaurants and other public places. Wilma grew up in this painful atmosphere of **racism** and **discrimination.** Many places in Clarksville were still segregated during her homecoming in 1960.

Wilma insisted that the parade should include everyone in town, both black and white. The celebration after the parade was the first **integrated** event in Clarksville. Both black and white people attended.

Dr. Martin Luther King Jr.

Baptist minister Dr. Martin Luther King Jr. (1929–1968) was a famous **civil rights** leader. He believed that everyone should be treated equally, no matter what their skin color was. He used only nonviolent ways to fight for civil rights for African Americans.

Dr. King, who was born in Georgia in 1929, led many parades and demonstrations in the 1960s. He helped to get passage of the Voting Rights Act of 1965. The law made it illegal to deny anyone the right to vote on the basis of race.

Dr. King was shot to death in Memphis, Tennessee, on April 4, 1968. But people still remember him. Today, every year, the nation honors Martin Luther King Jr. on the third Monday in January. This national holiday is Martin Luther King Jr. Day.

Wilma chatted with President John F. Kennedy at the White House in 1961. By the age of 21, she was already a famous Olympic runner and known throughout the world for her skill.

Chapter 7:
Wilma's Helping Hand

When Wilma Rudolph returned to the United States, she was greeted as a star. Everyone wanted to see her, to shake her hand. She took time off from school to travel and make appearances. Many people wanted her to speak to their group or organization. She met the mayor of Chicago and the president of the United States, then John F. Kennedy, in Washington. The Associated Press named her Woman Athlete of the Year for 1960. Wilma was the first woman ever to win the James E. Sullivan Award, which is given to the country's top amateur athlete.

Wilma was especially proud of being invited to run at the New York Athletic Club meet and at the Millrose Games in New York City in 1961. No woman had ever been asked to compete in these meets before. She tied her own world record for the 60-yard dash at the Millrose Games. She also won the Babe Didrikson Zaharias

Award for the best athlete of 1961. Many people believe that Didrickson, who died in 1956, was America's greatest female athlete.

Wilma returned to Tennessee State in 1962 at the age of 22 to finish her degree in elementary education. She knew the time had come to make a decision about her future. If she were to compete in the 1964 Olympic Games, she would have to stay in training the whole time. And she and her boyfriend Robert were talking about getting married.

Maybe, Wilma thought, it is better to go out on top. After all, she could not keep on winning every race forever. When she lost an indoor race in Los Angeles that year, the newspapers wanted to know what was wrong. Coach Temple thought that she was right about going out on top.

Wilma made her decision after a big meet in California in 1962. She won the 100-meter dash against Russian athletes and anchored the 400-meter relay team. But she had to come from behind to win that one. The crowd gave her a standing ovation and it was a sweet moment. But that was it, she thought. I am going out a winner. After the meet a little boy asked for her autograph. She not only signed his paper but gave him her track shoes as well. Wilma Rudolph, fastest woman in the world, had retired.

Babe Didrickson

Babe Didrikson Zaharias (1914–1956) has been called America's greatest female athlete ever. She was a great basketball and track and field star. Later in life she became an outstanding golfer.

Zaharias was born in Port Arthur, Texas. By 1930 she was a member of the women's All-America basketball team. Over the next two years, she won eight events and tied for a ninth in track and field. At the 1932 Olympic Games, she took gold medals for the 80-meter hurdles and the javelin throw. She would have won gold for the high jump too, but the judges outlawed the way she landed. In addition, "the Babe," as she was known, was excellent at baseball, softball, swimming, figure skating, billiards, and even football.

In 1932 the Babe started to play golf casually. She won the Women's Amateur **tournament** in 1946. The next year she won 17 golf championships in a row. In 1950 she was the U.S. Women's Open golf champion and again in 1954. Zaharias, who married professional wrestler George Zaharias in 1938, died of cancer in 1956. The Babe Didrikson Zaharias Award for the best U.S. female athlete honors her as one of the greatest athletes ever, and keeps her memory alive. The important award was won by Wilma Rudolph in 1962.

Wilma and Robert Ward had been married only a few months when this photograph was taken. Robert was also on the track team at Tennessee A & I University.

After retirement, Wilma went on two **goodwill trips,** one to Africa for the U.S. government and one to Japan for the Baptist Christian Athletes group. Sometimes a government or an organization will send athletes to perform in other countries. These are known as goodwill trips. She was gone for two months. When she returned, she was greatly saddened to learn that her first coach at her high school, Clinton Gray, had been killed in a car accident.

Marriage and graduation

That summer, Wilma married Robert, her childhood sweetheart. The wedding was held in a big open field because so many people wanted to attend. They would eventually have four children, Yolanda, Djuana, Robert Jr., and Xurry.

Wilma and her new husband did not go on a honeymoon trip because they could not afford to. In the 1960s Olympic athletes did not often earn a great deal of money from their fame. Wilma did not earn money from being the best. This was before athletes were offered large sums of money to sponsor, or advertise, shoes, clothing, and other products. She wrote, "people were always expecting me to be a star, but I wasn't making enough money to live like one." Today, top athletes sponsor products or go on tours that pay them very well.

Wilma received her diploma from Tennessee A & I University on May 27, 1963. Her mother attended the ceremony and was very proud of her Olympian daughter.

Wilma graduated from Tennessee State in 1963 at the age of 23. She accepted a job at Cobb Elementary School, which she once attended. Since childhood she had always wanted to be a teacher. She also coached Gray's track-and-field team at Burt High.

Wilma watched the 1964 Olympics without feeling sad that she was not part of it. She had a new life now.

A new life

After all her travels, small-town life did not appeal to Wilma as much as it once did. In 1965 the new family moved to a larger town in Evansville, Indiana, where Wilma was offered a job as director of a community center. The following year, they moved again to Poland Springs, Maine, so that Wilma could become head of a girls' physical education program sponsored by the federal government.

Then, in 1967 Wilma received a letter from then–Vice President Hubert Humphrey. He invited her to work with him in what was called Operation Champion. The project was to take inner-city students from the sixteen largest U.S. cities and give them sports training. The program wanted to offer sports training to teach these children how to get along with each other and work as a team. The vice president hoped sports training would also help keep them busy and out of trouble on the streets.

It was an especially important job at the time because so many American cities were in trouble. **Poverty** and **racism** had overtaken many large cities. President Lyndon Johnson had declared a "war on poverty." In addition, the struggle for equal rights in America was in full force. People were calling for equal treatment for all citizens. Some white people were fighting against this idea. Dr. Martin Luther King Jr., the great **civil-rights** leader, was assassinated in 1968. Many U.S. cities erupted in violenceand hatred over his murder and the fight for civil rights.

Wilma was eager to take part in Operation Champion. In the late 1960s, she traveled to various cities to help young people learn track and field and basketball. It was hoped that success in sports would help them out of poverty.

After Operation Champion, Wilma devoted her time to her family while working for numerous projects and **foundations.** She also supervised coaching programs at various colleges.

The Foundation

By this time, Wilma had worked hard and did not have money problems any longer. She continued to be in great demand around the country. She was a sports commentator on radio and television. In 1977 she published her autobiography, called *Wilma*, which was made into a movie for television. In 1980 she was elected to the Women's Sports Hall of Fame.

For a long time after the Olympic Games, however, Wilma felt that she was hired for jobs simply because she was famous. People wanted to use her name but did not really expect her to do anything. She wanted to be more than just a famous name. In 1982 she established the Wilma Rudolph Foundation.

The foundation was based in Indianapolis, Indiana, but there are now branches in many cities. Wilma wanted to help other young athletes of all ages to prepare for sports meets and for the Olympic Games. This **nonprofit** foundation was one of her greatest

Wilma stood next to race car driver Janet Guthrie at the Women's Sports Hall of Fame on September 16, 1980. Wilma was one of three women inducted into the hall that year.

achievements. **Nonprofit** means that the organization is not set up for the purpose of making money. It is usually supported by donations from private citizens or groups. The Wilma Rudolph Foundation helps any community schools in need, such as sending in tutors or buying books. It is still a successful organization today.

Wilma missed her family and her home state. In 1992 she placed a manager in charge of her foundation and moved back home to Nashville, Tennessee. There, she became a vice president of the Nashville Baptist Hospital.

Cancer

In 1994 shortly after her own mother's death, Wilma received awful news. She learned she had brain and throat cancer. She stopped appearing in public. Wilma did not want people to remember her as a sick person, but as a strong athlete. So she rarely left the house. Her close friend Coach Temple was one of the only people who could get her to leave the house. Sometimes, she walked arm-in-arm with him around the track.

Wilma was in and out of hospitals for several months. But, sadly, Wilma's disease was too far advanced to cure. On November 12 of that year, a few months after the diagnosis, Rudolph died at the age of 54.

All the honors

Many honors came to Wilma after her death. A bronze statue of her stands in her hometown of Clarksville. Tennessee State named a new dormitory and an indoor track for her. In 1997 the governor made June 23rd Wilma Rudolph Day in Tennessee.

Wilma Rudolph also received national awards. She was elected to the National Women's Hall of Fame award in 1994. She is also in the National Track and Field Hall of Fame, the U.S. Olympic Hall of Fame, and the Black Athletes Hall of Fame. She is the first woman to receive the National Collegiate Amateur Association (NCAA) Silver Anniversary Award, even though she competed before the NCAA sponsored women's championships.

Wilma Rudolph's short life was a triumph over pain, **poverty,** and **racism.** She became a winner by never quitting. She won honors as the fastest woman in the world. Today, she is remembered as a great American Olympic champion.

An inspiration

Wilma was a hero to many people, including African-American track stars Florence Griffith Joyner and Jackie Joyner-Kersee.

In 1988 Florence Griffith Joyner (1959–1998) became the first woman to win three gold medals since Wilma. In fact, Florence broke Wilma's world record time for the 200-meter. Her gold medal–winning time at the 1988 Olympics in Seoul, South Korea, was 21.34 seconds. Joyner died of heart problems in 1998.

Many consider Jackie Joyner-Kersee (b. 1962) to be one of the best all-around female athletes in the world. She has won six Olympic medals—three of them gold. Jackie said that she felt like Wilma was an old friend who was always in her corner. In 1998 Jackie retired from competing. She co-owns a car-racing team and runs her own foundation to help young children.

Glossary

anchor in relay races, the fourth and usually fastest runner on the four-member team who finishes the race

baton small rod passed between runners in relay races

civil rights personal freedoms guaranteed to all citizens by the U.S. Constitution

color barrier phrase used to describe barring people of different races from joining, for instance, an all-white club; used to describe the situation in professional baseball before Jackie Robinson joined the Brooklyn Dodgers

cross-country race of a certain distance held over open land

discrimination prejudice or unjust behavior to others based on differences in age, color, or gender

foundation organization established for a particular purpose, such as fighting poverty, cancer, or polio

goodwill trip trip or tours that are usually sponsored by the government or another organization, some good will trips send athletes to other countries to perform

integrate to join together people of all races; in the civil rights era, the act of bringing white and black people together in public places such as schools and restaurants

nonprofit organization set up for a purpose other than making profit (money), such as a reading program for children in a poor community; usually run by donations

polio feared disease of the early and mid-20th century marked by fever and paralysis. Dr. Jonas Salk produced a polio vaccine in 1953.

poverty having very little money or personal possessions

racism belief that one race is somehow better than another

relay race in which team members run a certain distance of the track and hand a baton to the next runner, who continues the race

scholarship money granted to a student by a college or foundation on the basis of excellence in academics, musical ability, or sports

segregated forcing people of different races to live apart from each other

therapist person trained to help people recover from mental or physical illness

trial race held prior to a main event, such as the Olympics, to decide which athletes are eligible

tournament championship series of games or athletic contests

vaccine medicine made of a weakened or killed disease-causing germ that when taken, helps prevent someone from catching the disease

Timeline

1940	Wilma is born in St. Bethlehem, TN, June 23.
1946	Wilma's leg is disabled from polio. Begins trips to Meharry Medical College, Nashville, for disabled leg.
1949	Wilma discards leg brace.
1952	Wilma joins the girls' basketball team at Burt High School.
1956	First AAU meet, Tuskegee, AL, Wilma loses all races; trains for Olympics at Tennessee State University; qualifies for trials in Seattle, WA; trains in Los Angeles; competes at Games in Melbourne, Australia, and wins bronze medal on **relay** team.
1958	Wilma graduates high school; wins **scholarship** to TSU.
1959	Wins at National AAU meet, Corpus Christi; qualifies at trials, Texas Christian University; trains at Kansas State University.
1960	Olympic Games, Rome. Wins 100- and 200-meter and 440 relay for three gold medals; called "fastest woman in the world.
1961	Wilma ties own 60-yard dash record at Millrose Games.
1962	Wilma decides to retire.
1963	Wilma graduates from TSU and marries childhood sweetheart.
1965	Wilma moves to Evansville, IN.
1966	Wilma moves to Poland Springs, ME.
1966	Wilma joins Operation Champion.
1977	Wilma's autobiography is published.
1980	Wilma is voted into Women's Sports Hall of Fame.
1981	Wilma establishes Wilma Rudolph Foundation.
1992	Wilma returns to Tennessee.
1994	Wilma is diagnosed with cancer; she dies November 12.

Further Information

Further reading

Anderson, *Dave. Story of the Olympics.* New York: Morrow, 2000.

Middleton, Haydn. *Ancient Olympic Games.* Chicago: Heinemann, 1999.

Middleton, Haydn. *Modern Olympic Games.* Chicago: Heinemann, 1999.

Savage, Jeff. *Top 10 Women's Sports Legends.* Berkeley Heights, NJ: Enslow, 2001.

Rutledge, Rachel. *The Best of the Best in Track and Field.* Brookfield, Conn.: Millbrook Press, 1999.

Sherrow, Victor. *Wilma Rudolph, Olympic Champion.* New York: Chelsea, 1995.

Addresses

National Women's Hall of Fame
76 Fall Street
P.O. Box 335
Seneca Falls, NY 13148
Write here for more information about Wilma.

Tennessee Sports Hall of Fame
   Museum
501 Broadway
Nashville, Tennessee 37203
Write here for a Wilma Rudolph trading card.

U.S. Olympic Committee
1750 East Boulder Street
Colorado Springs, CO 80909
Write here with your questions about the Olympics.

USA Track & Field
One RCA Dome, Suite 140
Indianapolis, IN 46225
Write here to learn more about the USA Track & Field team.

Index